word (wûrd), *n.* [A.S. < O.Teut. source], **1**, a sound, or combination of sounds, used in any language as a symbol of an idea, and forming a grammatical part of speech; a vocable; **2**, the printed or written letter or letters, or other characters, which represent the spoken word; **3**, speech; saying; remark; **4**, information; report; message; as, he received *word* of his mother's arrival; **5**, command; order; **6**, password; watch-word; **7**, affirmation; promise; as, he will keep his *word: pl.* **1**, conversation; as, not given to *words;* **2**, language used in anger or reproach; as, they had *words* yesterday: **Word**, *Theol.,* **1**, Christ considered as the expression of the Divine Intelligence and as the media-tor between God and men; the Logos; as, the *Word* was made flesh, and dwelt among us (John 1:14); **2**, the Scriptures: **word for word**, entirely, and in the very words; as, to repeat a conversation *word for word:—v.t.* to express in words.

WORDS

POETRY COLLECTION

BURT E. PRINGLE

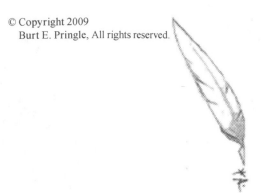

Printed in the United States of America.

A cataloguing record for this book that includes the U.S. Library of Congress Classification number, the Library of Congress Call number and the Dewey Decimal cataloguing code.

ISBN: 978-1-4269-3329-5 (sc)

Library of Congress Control Number: 2010906681

Order this book online at www.trafford.com
or email orders@trafford.com

Most Trafford titles are also available at major online book retailers.

 www.trafford.com

North America & international
toll-free: 1 888 232 4444 (USA & Canada)
phone: 250 383 6864 ♦ fax: 812 355 4082

TO RITA IPPOLITO

The sun travels through the day,
the moon traverses the night.
Let us be together and join them
in their flight.

I extend my heart-felt thanks to
Ms. Bronwen Chandler
for her expertise and assistance
in the editing of this collection of my poetry.

*I would also like to thank
all the people
who have come into my life
and have joined hands
to encircle me.*

"Do not
the most moving moments
of our lives
find us
without words."

Marcel Marceau
"BIP" The Mime

1923-2007

*

A NOTE FROM THE AUTHOR

I never plan to write and have no idea what
will come onto the page or how it will turn out
--- this I cannot explain. I only know I write
spontaneously, awake, or compose in my sleep
through a voice from my inner self. You may find
the diversity of these poems and vignettes
thought provoking and enlightening. They are
about the seasons that change our lives, our
relationship with God --- the joy and the pain,
of falling in love, departing, and the many
aspects of life (slices of life experiences, short
stories, if you will).
Some poems are direct and personal, others are
observations, pastoral, humorous, ever erotic
--- yet entertaining. You may find a message,
or a line that relates to your own life situations
that will lift your spirit or chill your heart.
Poetic lines might be discovered that come to life
and sparkle long enough to enjoy, for the written
word through time is full of these treasures.

May you also find these humble poetic efforts
of mine worthy of your time for I feel I am
God-blessed with this talent, and hope
your life will be filled with His blessings as well.

Always

Burt

Enjoy life, enjoy love, enjoy poetry !

CONTENT...

"Turn life into words."

GORE VIDAL

SILENT WORDS*

Come and read the lyrical line
from my very soul --- I wrote.
Dwell on the music caused
by each and every note.
'cause, silent is the written word
until read or sung or spoken
(or in one's heart, heard).
Then that silence will be broken.

*From my first book
My Never Ending Dance With Words

PAGES

The pages of time
--- left mildewed, faded and torn,
one written with heartache,
anguish and scorn.

What fate dealt you
can not be remembered or read
--- yet it is all stored somewhere
deep within your mind.

Someday, someone
will come into your life,
and those pages will turn
--- be exposed to the light,
removing the pain, the stresses,
the strife and the blight.

YESTERDAY'S SOULS

In a silent garden
rows of stones emerge from the fog
--- protruding sentinels that record
the names of yesterday's souls.
The ones who sort rest
from their toils and travels.
The ones who were anxious
to meet God on His own terms.

Yesterday's souls
--- lovingly remembered.

Moss laden oaks shelter
their artfully chisele'd monoliths
--- while night shadows loom
over stark white marble crypts.

A sudden breeze rakes the leaves
--- exposing the flowers left wilted,
unattended and forgotten.

3

FULFILLING MOMENT

In the silence of the morning
the air was filled with sweetness
as they lay embraced.
It was one of those enchanted nights
that left them breathless and content
in their still youthful hearts.

In the heat and sweat of the moment
shadows of the past faded,
tears dissolved,
inhibitions locked away
becoming one in heart and spirit
on their flight beyond ecstasy.

They had traveled long and dusty roads
of heartache and disappointment
to get there.

Now the moment is theirs.

SUMMMER DAZE

Smoldering, smothering,
simmering summer dazes
on this lonely road
--- stretched out before you.
Entranced by the mirage
of dancing heat
love walked through
its blinding glare
to approach you
--- playing tricks on your mind,
reviving forgotten memories
of another summer afternoon.

Love springing forth to entangle
you once more.

REED MUSIC

Cut a reed
from the water's edge
and carve a flute.
Press it to your lips;
through its hollow
heavenly music
will come forth
--- music emanating
from the heart.

DWELLING MUSIC

There is a song
*   that rings my ears*
*   and dwells within*
*   my heart.*
It is our love song
*   played night and day*
*   whether you're here*
*   or not.*

6

KNOWLEDGE

Dust gathering
  on a library shelf,
  no one there to read.
While its books
  lie dormant
  --- their pages hold
  all the knowledge
  and the seed.

VEILS

A bride vested all in white.
A widow's garment black.

Veiled so not to see their faces.

The blushing cheeks
--- the tear-filled eyes.

REALITY OF TIME

Oh how the tender years fly by
--- from a time when we built
all our hopes and dreams.
Then we are flung
into adulthood
where we are faced with
all that life brings forth
from its darkest corners
--- all the truths and illusions
we knew now shattered,
and the shards scattered
across life's floor.

As we grow older,
our bodies soften,
we become brittle,
our minds weaken
as we try to recapture
those tender years
now fragile, lost and forgotten.

LOVE/ROSE

ROSE, *it opens and blooms*
and thrusts its presence
into our lives.
We stand in awe at its beauty
and grandeur --- its perfect form,
its colour and fragrance.
It stays with us for a while
as we nurture it
every moment it exists,
then it folds, fades
and dies.

LOVE, *like that rose is beautiful.*
But remember,
there are always the thorns.

STIRRING INSIDE

Being with her
every day will be different,
undaunted, undeceived,
with an embracing heart.

You know you may be insane
and cannot help it
--- still something within
draws you closer to her
--- closer and closer
to a greater love.

You cannot begin the day
without offering
your prayers to her.
Your life would be lost
and inconsolable if she
were no longer there.

HOME AT LAST

On his way home
   he passed across
   rippling mountain streams
   and trekked through fields
   of golden blossoms
   that lay within his path.

When he arrives there'll be someone
   standing in an open door
   to welcome him,
   to end his way of wondering
   --- he'll be home at last.

*

HER TOUCH

When she touches him
and her loving and caring fingers
glide across his face
it turns his mind and body
into 'deepful' peace.
At one time only his soul
could have reached such peacefulness.
It is as if his heart is touched
by the softness of an Angel's wing
and he melts away.

SLIVER OF LIGHT

You can dispel the darkness
by lighting a single candle.
That sliver of light
parts the long
and lonely night.

SHADOWS

The moonlight shadows
form a lasting silhouette
of love against his heart
--- held by layers of time.

GAPING HOLE

Love has left a gaping hole
in his sanity and his life
has fallen through.

CYCLES

With summer love
do not delay,
--- for in the autumn
comes decay.

Through winter's wind
and blinding snow
your heart will pine,
for it will be empty
as once was mine.

Even memories fade
as time passes away.
Yet love will return
--- for another spring
is on its way.

SWEET KISSES

Silver wrappers on the floor.

She left a little white paper trail
*   to follow so I might go*
*   and find her sweet kisses.*

*

18 MILES WALKING

I told her I would walk
to the end of the earth for her.

She said, "start walking."

I won't have to go far
--- the Atlantic ocean
is only 16 miles away.

PLAY SWEET MUSIC,
SING SWEET SONGS

The moment we met
I became lost
in the music
emanating from my heart.

She is the treasure
that enriches my life.
Only God
could have given her
that precious presence
and allowed my heart
to sing such sweet songs.

I asked her to dance
through life with me.
Partners, friends, lovers
we shall be.

SUN/MOON/STARS

She is the sun, his first glimpse of day.
She is the moon on its nightly rounds,
the stars that come out each night
--- brilliantly bright.

She is the love that captured his heart.

HEARTSTONE

Her name is etched in stone
and that stone is now heavy
in his heart since the day she left.

Heavier than one could ever know.

Every day when the sun breaks dawn,
his love will still be with her
--- wherever she may go.

AFRAID TO SPEAK

Her body, filled with desire
and a warm, soft glow
--- heart beating rapidly
as she tries to tell him something,
but her lips will not let go.

He strains to listen
--- there is a pain that persists
for he cannot hear those words.

Still her heart is afraid to speak.

Oh, how he longs to hear those words.

SOJOURNER ?

The dark clouds of longing were lifted
and a bright new dawn had arrived
bringing a new love to you
on silent wings.
With fulfillment in your heart
--- the sojourn begins.

Will it go beyond the allotted time ?

*

DAY

The silhouetted trees
    bow to the gentle breeze
    and dance with joy.
Velvet clouds
    --- sun on rise.
Grass nourished by the dew
    --- life renewed.

Morning glow.

LOVE'S TAVERN

I lived in a sober way
until love came and offered me
her wine and I became
completely drunk.

My heart stagger'd and cried
--- more wine,
*   more wine.*
I heard her sweet, soothing voice
--- more wine,
*   more wine*
I was warmed by her smile
--- more wine,
*   more wine.*
I felt the beat of her amorous heart
--- more wine,
*   more wine.*
I saw passion in her eyes
and begged for more wine.

When the time comes
they'll have to drag my dead body
from her tavern
--- until then,
I will be constantly drunk.

SONG

He sings a song
   composed from the feelings
   deep in his heart.
To her he sang this song
   --- but it seemed to fall
   deafly on her ears.

Awaken the heart to this music.
It unfolds the truth and the love
   his heart holds.
Open those eyes that have constantly
   shed the tears, to reveal the stars
   hidden within.

For this wall that was built
   casts a long shadow,
   and is covered with clinging vines
   that still grow from the roots
   planted in the past.

Remove the barrier and cluttering vines.
Let everything come to light.
Let his song waft through her heart,
   engulfing her and bring her
   a new joy --- a love
   that will endure.

ON THE WANE

All-encompassing was the love
he tried to extend to her
in the hour of his waning madness.
He still doesn't comprehend
what fate wanted to bestow on them.

As he touched the rosiness
of her cheek --- they spoke,
reminding him of a lost passion;
it grew to re-ignite a single ember
left smoldering in his heart
only she could have fulfilled his longing
during the days and nights
of his loneliness.

Now images of her are burned
into his mind.
Echoes of his lost love ricochet
off the walls of his empty heart.

SEARCHING FOR ANSWERS

He reads what's on her face.
He searches deep within her eyes
to find her --- yet she is not there,
her mood always changing
--- changing like a chameleon.

How can he keep up with her ?
How can he focus, gaze deep within ?

He hopes that she is not a wanderer,
a searcher, a seeker trying to find
the answer to longing
for it is not out there, it is within.

UNDYING LOVE IN ASHEN STONE

As I entered the chapel
a lone stained-glass window
offered a kaleidoscope of colour
to its dimly lit interior.
Ignoring the stone rubbers at work
with their papier and chalk
I came across two effigies
side by side --- a titled pair,
cloaked in majesty and mystery.
A knight with his sword
lying lengthwise his torso
and a princess sculptured
in proper dress of the time,
his ungloved hand touching hers
--- captured in permanent repose
--- in ashen stone
by an unknown sculpture's
chisel and keen eye for detail.
The Latin inscription, now worn over time,
 yet readable.

"THEY LIVED, THEY LOVED,
NOW THEY SLEEP. SLEEP
THEIR ETERNAL SLEEP TOGETHER."

--- together in a chapel vault below.

Someone across time
still places a single rose
on their hands in remembrance
of their undying love.

31 DECEMBER

Today is the last day, another year
comes to an end.
Another year "Gone With The Wind."
Will love descend or ascend ?
Will a new life begin or this one end ?

*

LEGACY

The past is full of voices
calling out to you,
wanting you to remember
their legacy.

STATUESQUE

Come into love's garden
   and close the gate behind
   for there will be no reason
      to decline.
Stroll the cobbled pathway
   down to where
   the purple lilacs grow.
There you will find true love
      waiting,
wearing a crown of stars
   and moonlight shining
   on her hair:
a mystifying beauty,
   more than one's eyes
   or heart can bear.

With great expectations
   the veiling mist of evening
      begins to clear,
   exposing her alabaster figure,
   with perfectly sculptured
   breast and hips
   and love's sweet nectar
   waiting on her lips.
But she is only
   an entrancing marble beauty
      --- a statue.
Its model and your true love
   is standing in the near.

ON A SOUTHERNLY NIGHT

Some say,
"There is madness in moonlight."

A full moon rises on a cloudless
southern sky. The night air, thick
with the perfume of honeysuckle
as they stroll through the French doors
onto the veranda.
The silhouetted trees frame the night.
Spanish moss --- like liquid silver
dripping from their branches
in the moonlight.
A canopy of ebony velvet
holds a multitude of stars
--- adding to the enchantment.

At the balustrade she said,
"linger here with me awhile
and tell me that you love me
--- surrender your heart to me
before the dawn,
for I want to love you
through this heavenly night."

His voice choked in reply;
"You know I live in your presence,
I dwell in the depth of your eyes.
You know my heart is filled with you
* --- so why do you ask ?*

Let us take this night and fill our hearts
with the magic and the madness
that this southern night ensures,
and maybe we'll survive the dawn."

TOAD

After all the time he spent in pursuit,
*   he has come to the end of the road,*
for she never offered him that kiss
*   to make him her prince charming*
*   --- so he will just remain a toad.*

SHARDS

Love's shattered dreams
and broken heart:
those bits and pieces
and the remains of life
--- the winds of hope
have blown away.

Burt Quote:
"Tears embrace life's sorrows."

TIME PASSENGERS

We are passengers in time
as the years slip by
season after season.

Like the birds that fly south
in the winter,
only to return
as spring fills the air
--- taking flight
to go home again.

But desperately as we try
--- we can not go back home
or live that time again.

Even if we could,
nothing would ever
be the same.

HER HAUNTING EBONY EYES

What is behind those ebony eyes,
*   holding secrets yet untold ?*
Sometimes warm, sometimes cold
*   --- penetrating --- cutting a path*
*   deep into his soul.*
So dark, so mysterious those eyes,
*   blacker than the midnight skies.*

What will they reveal to him ?

Ebony eyes, stressed with pain
*   --- not to cry, not to tear.*
What are those secrets
*   she has to fear ?*
Her eyes taunt him
*   as he closes his to sleep.*
Her eyes haunt him
*   even in his dreams.*

Only love can soften those ebony eyes.

Her ebony eyes
   with love a-blazing,
exotic, hypnotic --- he is entranced
   by her ebony gazing.

He hears "I love you"
   whispering through his mind.
He feels it in his heart.
He sees it in her eyes.
He longs to hear it from her lips.

THE SILENT ONES

Sitting 5th row, center
--- Saturday night in the dark.
Life and shadows
flicker across the screen
in black and white
(some times tinted in sepia or blue
to heighten the mood).

Funny men with their slapstick
and "prat-falls" --- you don't hear a sound,
except for the laughter,
a "rim-shot," a drum roll
--- the music coming from a pit up front
interpreting the action.
Actor's with operatic jesters,
mouthing words trying to emulate
the legitimate stage they were born to.
The silence of speech --- that we interpret
or read as it appears on screen
to keep us up to date --- fill us in
--- leavening us speechless as well.

Do we ever wonder what was really said ?

A silent epic reels on
through that streak
of Edison's light overhead
that gives us an out, an escape
into another world for awhile.

Ground-breaking moments in celluloid,
weaving the tapestry of our imagination
with colossal productions to treat the eye
--- film noir, drama, dark and mysterious.
Camera's applying all "the tricks of the trade,"
two small figures, waltzing or clashing swords
as their overly dramatiz'd shadows
fill the screen, a close-up kiss or being caught
in the middle of a western stampede.

We leave the theatre mumbling words
under our breath as if we were
the celluloid people --- the silent one's.

"YOU WANT FRIES WITH THAT ?"

The night is ablaze with neon
flashing yellow, red and blue
--- the familiar Logos of our time,
enticing us to their troth.
To our feeding of fat, calories
and cholesterol.
Our obsession, our need
for "fast food."
Our passion for burgers and fries
from their sizzling, greasy grills.
Pull down the lever,
all the bubbling soda you can drink
--- refills, no extra charge.
Drive in, drive out
or stand in line at the counter
to surrender
our hard earned cash.
Maybe slip across the street
to the Queen for a royal dessert,
or have those round platters of cheesy
dough with your favorite toppings
delivered to your door.
Heartburn, 30 minutes or less.

Not to leave out all that fried chicken
with its famous recipe.

I never knew buffalo's had wings
until I found I could buy them
by the bucket full.

AFTER LOVE'S SILENT DAWN

After the night
that had taken them
to heights never before obtained,
came the silence of the dawn.
Her soft, warm body nestled in his arms,
her saintly face resting on his shoulder
and her long silken tresses
draped across the pillows.
He watched her heaving breast
as she slept --- rising and lowering
with every breath.

It was a sweet and silent dawn
--- two heartbeats resonate
in the dim morning light.

Then, surprisingly she up-rose
that morning on unconfined wings
and flew toward the rising sun
--- like a swan lifting from stilled waters,
leaving only her shadow
and a lasting ripple on his heart.

DAILY PRAYER

Dear God,
Thank You for another day.

May I find joy throughout this day
and may she feel this enjoy as well.

May Your blessings be upon us
and may we all live together
as one earth family.

May peace reign on this earth,
so everyone can love and worship
in Your name.

In Your name, Amen.

Burt Quote:
"Look not with your eyes but with your heart."

A LOVER'S PRAYER

Lord, give me the wind
to billow my sail.
Give me a star
to chart my way.
Give me her heart
that we may journey
together in love.
Give me the strength
to make it endure.
Give us the heart
to follow our dreams.

Amen

SKYLAKE

So clear, so calm,
the lake became a reflected sky.
A panoramic view of the Heavens,
as the clouds seem to skim
just below the surface,
undaunted by the tree images
along the shoreline.

The pin-drops of spring rain came
turning into circles,
circles ever expanding
trying to reach the shore
before they fade.

Then once again
--- so clear, so calm,
so peaceful --- God's skylake.

OFFERING

He offered his hand
to her healing.

He opened his heart
for her comfort.

He offered his days and nights
toward her care.

He placed his love
at her altar
so they could be together.

She said once;
 " her plate was full."
He said;
"Let me make it overflow."

O' LOVE OF MINE

O' love of mine
--- now wandering,
where have you gone ?

The shadows
have claimed you.
The moon hides you
behind a veil.
Come out of the darkness
--- free of your wanderings
and be safe once more
in the arms of love.

MY ROSE

You are the one rose in my garden,
and you adorn my garden with beauty.
Your sweet fragrance
has my heart spellbound.
But there is an agony of yearning,
for the thorns keep us apart.

Leaves may wither
and the stem bend and weaken,
but I'll never let the bloom
fade from my rose.

May the Lord allow my garden
to always be graced by you.

NIGHT FIRE

We heard the beautiful sound
of the nightbird's song
as our hearts merged
in the nocturnal light
along our garden path.

We felt the heat
as love set aflame
our hearts
--- and the roses.

Burt Quote:
"Love is the call of the day
        while lust addresses the night."

TANGO

Come fly with me
down to Argentina
where the warm summer nights
will embrace us.
We will dance the tango
as the natives do,
under a canopy of flirting stars.

Slow, sensuous, seductive.

There isn't a more intriguing sound
than tango,
full of passion and desire.
Yet, it has frailty and strength
--- to cling to, to dance to
as feet move in swiftness, slowness,
step by step, curling and swirling
to the intoxicating rhythm
of the drum's pulsating beat,
the violin's haunting strands,
rippling accordions, strumming guitars,
and a tango singer's passion-filled voice
penetrating our rapturous night.

THREE NAILS

Where are the hand-forged nails
that pierced Him ?
Do they lie somewhere
covered by time,
rusting in the ground
(now made holy by His blood)
--- never to be found ?

Look into your soul,
where they might lie dormant
--- ready to materialize,
fresh from the blacksmith's forge
and the cross.
Let your heart know the pain,
the cruel death He endured for you
--- live in the joy of His glorious rise.

Three nails = Faith --- Hope --- Love.

THE DREAM ?

I dreamed I walked
into a Carpenter's shop;
doves were perched
on the rafters cooing.
Sun rays penetrating the cracks
of its aged timbered walls
--- reverence abounded in this
work place.

There He stood in a garment
of pure light
with a mallet and chisel
in His hand --- hewing cedar wood
(as if carving His own cross).
His sandaled feet standing
in the wood shavings
and the dust of ages.
I felt too, the Father was there
but could not be seen.

I approached,
He put out His hand
to receive me.

All was at peace.

When I woke there was
wood dust on my hand.

45

SPEAK AN EVENING PRAYER

At sunsets most beauteous moment
when the sky is ablaze with colour
--- ask the Lord to slow your pace
so you might gather your thoughts,
and leave life's trials behind.

Let the tranquility of the night prevail
and your heart be stilled
from all earthly troubles.

Let the gentleness of His love
take you peacefully into sleep
to rest, to rise once more,
like the sun, to shine
in the new day.

SACRED SANDALS

Jesus wore sandals
--- crafted by an unknown cobbler's
loving hands not knowing
the divine footsteps they would take.

The leather strong, yet supple that graced
His feet for comfort and support.
Hard worn over time
--- they lived up to their task
during His short tenure here on earth.

That sacred pair still supported Him
as He struggled with the cross
on the way to Calvary.
Then they were bartered by the soldiers
for the highest price.

Precious are the feet that they adorned.
Precious in our hearts is the man
who wore them.

Let us slip into a pair of sacred sandals
and also walk His way.

TO MY QUEEN

*He clinker his glass and said
vociferously;*

*"I propose a toast to my Queen
for she brightens my kingdom
with love's everlasting light."*

*

BREAKFAST

*He placed a rose
on her breakfast tray
and entered her chamber.
She set-up in bed
with her dreamy eyes
and he kissed her
       "good morning"
placing the tray on her lap.*

*As the sun began to rise
he slipped beside her
--- time seemed inert
as their hearts beat together
and in the morning quietude they
prepared to meet the new day.*

TO MY LOVE

The King of England
had no greater love,
than the love I have for you.

I have not a throne to advocate,
or regal crown to share.
I only have a loving heart
to give to you my dear.

I ask you now for your hand,
so soft and fair,
to marry me and live with me
--- my destiny is clear.
I want to love and cherish you,
and forever have you near.

PEARL OYSTER

He lifted her from the sea of uncertainty,
  opened her shell to reveal
  a perfect sphere, a perfect gem
  --- a lustrous pearl
  embedded in her succulent flesh.

He placed that pearl
  on an altar to worship.

The shell, her past, he left on the beach
  to be washed away with the tide.

SEA SHELL

From the sea of despair
--- like a shell washed ashore,
resting on a beach --- alone.

Bleached and dried --- the sun,
blazing down when she found him
--- she brushed away time's sand
and took him home
to love and care for --- but then
he found she only wanted
to add him to her collection.

Throw him back into the sea
--- maybe someday he'll find
the right beach.

OPENING HEART

She opened his heart
to the joys a new love would bestow
--- though time had locked its door.
She opened his heart to a love
--- never felt before.
She opened his heart
and now it's hers
--- forevermore.

DELIGHTED HEART

My cup, filled to the brim,
for the fruit of love has ripened
and the taste delights my heart
--- it's wine has consumed me.

You are my sunshine
--- my precious one
I linger here in your golden rays
of promise.

BOSOM MEMORIES

The dearest things in life
  he holds
  deep within his heart:
Her name, their time,
  the moments shared:
The love
  that fell away.

Though he has lost
  and she have gone away,
  no more their dance,
  --- their song to play.
He'll hold these memories secure
  within his bosom
  until his final day.

THE TREE HOUSE

Her father built an elaborate tree house
for her mother, magnificent to see,
so on rainy afternoons they could go
and be together and love.

They would be out there for hours,
embraced in rapture,
eternal lovers among the showers.

The old oak, huge, its branches
cascading far and wide;
it was there they knew each other,
their passions not to hide.

The tree house, painted white
with columned veranda, long and wide,
nestled in the branches --- and
painted in colours of love inside.

The earth would tremble,
the branches shake
from the vibrations
their ecstasy of love would make.

When she was a child she would go out
to the tree house, sit alone and dream
about a love that was meant to be.

The 'ole plantation style and that era
--- "gone with the wind."
This big and beautiful tree house
--- the legacy they handed down to her,
so love and passion might again
live within the tree.

Now in her true love's embrace
She said,
"The rain is coming down,
the thunderous roar --- inviting
by its sensuous sound.
You are my darling, you my love
I will not deprive --- come out
to the tree house and make love to me.
There we will keep the beauty
and the memory of their love
and passion alive."

YOUTH REVIVED

They stood naked
in body and soul,
locked in love's embrace.
It seemed as if
a block of time
had been lifted
and they were young again.

She with a radiant glow
--- he with an exuberant heart
waiting for the next moment
with heart-felt expectation.

All inhibitions swept away
as they lie in each other's arms
fulfilling their greatest desires.

With the warmth of the day
diminishing and with twilight's
final flicker --- night descends
and they are lost
in that blissful moment
of surrender.

CONQUERED TIME

The hour glass's sand
ceased to shift
and time was locked
in the moment.

They stepped outside themselves
at the height of ecstasy,
and saw two young lovers
in passion's embrace.
Gone were the marks of time
on their faces
--- he looked young again
as did she, lying there next to him.

The shadows of the past
--- diminished, for their love
had conquered time.

HAUNTING MEMORIES

Tears freely flow from his eyes
--- gladdened that love is still alive
and not dead:
Tears full of salt and memories
of the life he once led.

There was a time in his life
he lived without a goal.
Then love came to shine on him
and the mysteries of life
began to unfold.

With a once-clogged brain,
and once-closed mind
--- memories still haunt him
from time to time.

LOVE and LOVE LOST

His life is full, but empty
 because you are gone
 from him today.
So, his heart has stored
 all the memories
 that will brighten
 his darkened way,
 and he shall always love you,
 each long and lonely day.

Because,
 there are some things
 time cannot erase,
 'cause he can slip into
 his secret place
 where memories live
 and his loves anew
 to relive the time
 he shared with you.

CESSATION

The light that shone on his love
--- now extinguished.
The promises that held
his heart together --- now gone.
The cold winds of winter
have blown away the memories
that were the staples of his life.

The stars have lost their luster,
the moon has slipped behind a veil
and the nights are dark.
The eerie silence of the wind,
the thick air: there is a nothingness
that now prevails in his life
--- his world, spinning out of orbit.

GOLDEN YEARS, GOLDEN LOVE

At a time when many only exist
through long, lonely days
and chilling nights
--- they found each other.
Hearts now quickly beat
with a new passion's heat.

She is still beautiful and desirable
in these golden years.

There is no rush now.
Their bodies worn by time
--- they undress in subdued light.
Everything done with ease,
the embrace, the kiss,
the gentle caresses.
How sweetly they love.
Wandering down pathways
long remembered,
yet not traveled in years.

As the hour-glass's sand
slowly sifts away
they hold on to every breath
--- cherish every moment
as if it were their last.
They find no time to weep
but live and love today,
for tomorrow may only bring
death and decay.

GOD'S IMAGE

We are all "made in God's image."

If we keep killing His images
--- someday there won't be any
of God's images left.

GRASSHOPPER

The grasshopper
plays its music like a bow
crossing violin strings.

How beautiful its song
that must fade away
as fall approaches.

CAPPUCCINO

She is like dark brewed coffee,
brown complexion glistening,
shimmering, reflecting her soul.

Memories of her ancestors
with their sweat and toil
silently still live in her heart.
Realizing her past has made
possible her future
---free to be herself, to strive
and conquer against all odds.

The unforgivable past,
forgivable in this generation
because the colour of one's skin
does not matter. It's what
lies within that counts.

Now she stands tall today
with all of life's changes
mentally, physically and spiritually
--- challenging herself
in this modern world.

KIDNAPPED

His heart has been kidnapped,
  his love held for ransom.

Others may have had
  more worldly worth
  to barter with than he
  --- he has no treasures to bestow.
He can only lie at her feet,
  a gift for her taking
  --- his only possession --- his heart,
  wrapped up in devotion
  and a pledge of undying love.
For he has no fear of commitment,
  his only joy is in his anticipation.

Burt Quote:
"If you had everything,
there would be nothing more to receive
or new rewards given."

DISQUIETED HEART

Sometimes you have sunshine.
Oft-times you get rain
--- and when it rains
a dark, cloudless sepia sky,
a gray and failing moon
--- those illusive stars
lose their shine.

Left is a disquiet'd heart
when dreams begin to fade
--- a world that exists
after love has been
torn away.

WAITING AT HIGH NOON

He waits for her
across a fresh green meadow
--- beneath a Sycamore tree.
The sun is at high noon
--- its downward shadow
casts a cooling silver-blue shade
through spring's full boughs.

The day is fine. The sky is blue
--- a bird somewhere on high
is still chirping its morning song
as he sits and waits for her.

Even his waiting is sweet
for his heart is filled with her.

ENDLESSLY HE WAITS

He waited for her to come
--- 'til the trees lay bare
and winter's snow began to fall.
Oh, how long he waited
--- but she never came at all.

Now a new sun is bursting forth
and everything starts to bloom.
How much longer must he wait ?
I guess,
until his enduring heart
becomes love's tomb.

MIRROR, MIRROR

They share the same birth-time.
They have passed through the same hours
not knowing who they were
or where they were going
--- until now.

They are mirrors, soul mates.

They look at each other
and see themselves in many ways.
They both have been down that road
of heartache and despair
--- surviving many of life's
destructive times.

They have come together
in a heart-searching moment
where they can now find
fulfillment and lost dreams
--- that "silver lining"*
that makes plain glass reflective.
That silver lining is theirs to grab
--- to hold onto and reflect
an image of one.

They are mirrors, mirrors,
to look into each other
and see themselves.

*Silver amaign

CHASING DREAMS

In a lonely bed
   his dreams to chase,
full of memories
   of love's embrace
   --- memories
   that cannot be replaced.
He wishes the night
   didn't go by so fast
   --- so a little longer
   his dreams would last.

He lies in the quiet
   of a Sunday morn
   hugging his pillow
   --- since she has gone.

He longs to hold her
   in a lover's bed
   --- but for now, that dream
   lives in his head.

MIDNIGHT LOVE

He opened the door
and there she stood
in all her awesome beauty.
Into his outstretched arms she came,
they locked in a lover's embrace.
Their minds had but one thought:
to fly away into the night
to places unknown
for rapture had captured them
with a single breath.

It's midnight as smoke curls
from a candle --- just snuffed out.
All inhibitions are thrown to the winds
as they peeled away time
and their modest coverings.
Her warmth, not cooling
like the candles' wax
but searing in his hands.
He lifts her up
carrying her to bed.

The sweet scent of jas'min
fills the night air
--- the soft glow of a full moon
streams through
the partly opened shutters
and across their joining.

Now the moment stood still
--- time was lost as if they were
the only ones in existence,
with their passion clinging to the hour.

Midnight --- moonlight --- love.

CRISIS

My life in crisis.
No shoes.
　No booze.
　　No chews.
　　　No wo's.
　　　　No smooze.
　　　　　No snooze.
　　　　　No dues
　　　　　　No news.
　　　　　　No clues
　　　　　　　--- I lose.

Burt Quote :
"When you grow up with nothing
everything becomes something."

COOL CAT

Over the fence and down the alley
* --- green eyes glarin', searchin'*
* for that one sweet kittie named Sally.*
Struttin' as only he knows how
* --- night-mist softens*
*   his lusty meow-ou.*
That back porch Romeo
* --- didn't have far to go.*
Tom cat prowlin' the night
* finds that feline in his sight.*

She too, was out for the night
* --- her fur coat gleamin'*
* in the bright moonlight.*
She was a-purrin',
* no claws were showin'*
* --- ready for Freddie,*
* the coolest cat in town.*

Four paws softly pat the ground,
careful not to make a sound.
Slippin' back on the back porch,
* curlin' up in a corner*
*   --- out of sight,*
* dreamin' of another*
*   love filled night.*

SILENT MIST

The silent mist of morning
brings the tears that linger
on the lush green meadow
as dew.
It forms the raindrops
that nourish the earth
--- then becomes
the crystal flakes of snow
to turn everything
into a majestic
winter portrait.

SILENT REFRAIN

The morning air is filled
with bird songs.
But there is another song
only you can hear
floating on the wind.

That lost heart-song's
silent refrain.

HEARTS IN AGE

Hours before they sleep
they take their evening stroll
--- still holding hands,
still holding hearts in age
as that ole moon
trudges across the night sky
--- aglow with its antique shine.

The rewards of mutuality prevail
--- there is no sadness or strife
in their lives.
With tenderness and compassion,
love is the driving force
in this companionship
--- there is much they say
without a word spoken.

As late night approaches
they lift a glass of wine
to toast the day
and all its blessings
--- a prayer,
then the warmth of each other
sustaining them in slumber
--- to rise again as one
at another day's beginning.

MOONGLOW

Blue-black is the night
and the soothing calm
it delivered.

The night clouds
sail across the sky
trying to obscure the moon,
yet its light still breaks
to expose its fullness
as the star Venus
"slides-up" to its side,
and young lovers reach
into the darkness
--- illumed
only by the moon.

FEBRUARY MORNING

The morning fog
lays a thin veil across
a dew-fresh meadow.
The moon still dominates the sky
--- as the sun's on rise
to burn away the night.

Long streaks of light filter
between the silhouetted trees
causing the back-lit pines
to cast long shadows
--- like prison bars across the ground
as if trying to keep
the peacefulness of morning
from escaping.

NOCTURNE

A full moon waltzes
  with veils of meandering clouds
  as stars are dancing
  to some celestial song.
The cosmic rhythm
  set in motion causes the earth
  to sway to and fro.
Mystical music,
  it is as silent as the night
  yet lover's hear
  with great delight.
It fills the air
  with nocturnal love
  --- delights their hearts
  and fills their lives
  with joy.

RAIN

The explosive sound
of God's heavenly cannons roar
with its continual rumbling roll
--- lightning rips across the sky
with those blinding streaks of light.
Clouds turn a doleful gray,
and the sun runs for cover
--- so do the birds.
Soon there will be rain
to wash away the grime
and replenish the earth.

The clouds will diminish,
the sky turn a soft, subtle blue
and a rainbow will replace the rain
--- God's promise.

GOD'S BREATH

I listen to the rush of the wind
through the trees
at vesper-time.
I sense it is God's breath
reassuring me of His presence
--- and I know
I can peacefully sleep
cradled in His arms.

*

THE CENTER

The high point of my soul
is where God lives:
Where spirituality flows:
Where time and movement will stop
and become the stillness of eternity.

ASLEEP IN HIS ARMS

Reality slips away
into unconsciousness.
The memory of her comforts his soul
for she was his many seasons of joy
--- the moments he will cherish
with a lonesome heart
--- knowing
her earthly body is still
and she is resting in peace.

Asleep in God's arms tonight.

*

WELL OF TEARS

In grief,
the eyes well with tears
and from that welling
we draw strength
--- knowing others
share our pain
of loss.

To Samuel Panto
In memory of his beloved Jane.

BORN, THE CHRIST, THE KING

Over a stable
a star shone bright,
to guide men there
on that holy night.

Simple shepherds,
wise men three,
all came to worship
on bended knee.

To praise His birth
as Angels sing
to bring glad tidings
of The Christ, The King.

God's only son
in human guise,
who came to us
from beyond the skies.

To lie in a manger
--- now His throne,
we know His sacrifice
when He was grown.

Born to save
our wretched soul,
as taught to us
from pages old.

We celebrate now
with trees of light,
The Christ, His glory
and His earthly flight.

So, come one, come all
to the stable door
and raise your voices
--- your love to show.

That The Christ, The King
was born this day:
There rejoice,
kneel and pray.

Then peace be with you
--- one and all,
for all shall answer
His final call.

YOU and I

You walked with me
*   when I was lonely.*
Comforted me
*   when I was frightened.*
Consoled me
*   when I needed care.*
Showed me the right path
*   when I needed direction.*
You reached out and took my hand
*   when I was lacking confidence.*
You were always there for me
*   --- even when I strayed.*

You are the source of my light
*   and the promise of eternal life.*

Burt Quote :
"With tomorrow comes a fresh new start."

MY ROCK

I dwell under the shadow
of my rock.
It soothes and cools me
in the summer heat
--- shields me from
the winter storms.
My rock can also be
your rock
--- "The Rock of Ages"
that we sing.
For He is my rock
who protects
and comforts me
--- keeps me safe
from harm.

So come and sit
under the shadow
of "The Rock" --- the one
that comforts me.

"He alone is my rock
and my salvation."
PSALMS 62:6

YOUR SONG

There are other songs
to dance to but this one
is all your own --- your song.
You try to retrieve every word
as they drift out
into the evening air.

You dance in close embrace,
dreaming, as time fades away
and you are left together
in another world
as they play your song.

CHEEK TO CHEEK

The night was full of enchantment.
Music and a breath of fragrance
from the hyacinths filled the air.

Through the open French doors
you could see them slow-dancing
out on the veranda
--- the dim-lit lanterns were also
swaying in a misty rain.

They said, "they were crazy."

They're not crazy
--- just love entwining two hearts
as they dance in the rain.

"WINDY" JONES

She is his "Windy" Jones
--- talks a lot,
not quiet for a mo,
always talking about something
everywhere they go.
Talk, talk, talking,
mostly about nothing.

Always immersed in conversation
for talking is her game.
Words seem to spill off her tongue
like a cascading waterfall
--- but he loves her just the same.

She is his "Windy" Jones.

WIFE SHOPPING

He went out "wife-shopping"
and found and fell in love
with her
--- hoping she comes with
a lifetime guarantee.

TIMELESS HEART

Love, desire, passion,
always echoing through
the chambers of his heart;
its walls weakened by time
--- by Cupid's arrows
yet it still beats
suppressing all the bruises,
aches and pains
--- the grief, the remorse
and the endless longing
 --- then he found her.

REMEMBERING

When your heart is broken
and you have lost your will,
the quiet moments of remembering,
linger with you still.
Of all the joys and sorrows,
the happiness and the strife
--- all the things you shared with her
when she was in your life.

So, may your heart always be light
--- your soul free as a butterfly.
Keep God in your life,
love and joy in your heart.

Remember !

Wherever she goes
she will linger in your thoughts.
Wherever you go
she will always be in your heart.

SUMMER WIND

Drive on --- sing
and play your song
summer wind,
as we dance
through the soothing rain
to meet a coming rainbow.

*

I HEARD THE WIND

I heard a surge of wind come up
just before the wind chimes
began to play.
Resounding notes
in rich melodic tones
as the strikers sway
and randomly strike
the hollow metal tubes;
the glass prisms of another
wind chime tinkle in duet
on a quiet Sunday morning.

Heavenly sounds
to those who listen.

NEW BEGINNING

My thoughts
  have gone wild,
because into my life
  she brought a smile:
A smile that wasn't
  there before.

She charmed me,
  lifted my spirit
  and put my life on "go".
With love in my heart
  and my soul set free,
  everything in life has
  new meaning to me.

It let me know
  that my life needed her
  --- and I found that she
  needed me too.

THE "PIANO" BOYS

We were just kids
and were not concerned
about our different colours.
I was the white keys
and he was the black
--- we laughed and played
youth's wonderful music together
--- and it was sweet.
Then someone came
and spoiled it all
saying, "thy shall not meet."

And were separated, segregated.

So I grew up in Burt's world
and Ivy was retained in his
--- but we will always be
brothers under the skin,
no matter where he is today.

If fate has its way
one day we will meet
and play our music's
last refrain.

ABUNDANT DAY

There is a prelude to morning
--- black clouds against
a steel-blue sky slowly merging
with a pink glow on the horizon.

I know my new day is coming
and it will be full of all the abundance
life has to offer
--- spiritually and materially,
because I am well aware
of my source.

Burt Quotes:

"With self-yeast rise."

"Time is always chipping away
pieces of life."

LOVE ON A CAROUSEL

As they stood there
  in the middle of the room
  so tightly embraced
  with that one lasting kiss
  --- everything was passing so swiftly.
Walls were crumbling
  all around them.
The natural fears and anguish,
  the nerviness, hesitation and
  forethought were loosing ground
  for the evening air was full of desire.
He wanted to lift her in his arms
  and take her to bed
  --- but he was afraid, afraid
  after all those years of abstinence
  he would disappoint her
  --- still it has been in many ways
  their connecting day.

Let this love be a ride,
  like the one on a carousel
  --- enchanted, exciting and fun,
  and its music will endlessly play.
True, it will have its ups and downs
  and something seems to be going
  around in a circle --- going nowhere.
But that will only be momentary,
  because life is sweet
  and they will ride off
  into a beautiful sunset together.

THE WANDERER

The dark clouds of night
have concealed their moon
--- an awesome, yet haunting sight.

He gathered the stars in clusters
for a lantern --- following the path
laid out by the Milky Way
--- transcending the unknown.
The murmuring galactic winds
seem to whisper her name.

She is like a fiery star Nebula
burning in his soul as he goes wandering
--- searching to find a way
back to her heart.

VOYAGEUR

With your compass needle twirling
you sail not east nor west
--- but above into the firmament.
There are no directions to follow
except God's path.
The stars become your guide
through mystic clouds, cosmic storms
and celestial clusters,
leaving this galaxy to arrive
in a vortex ever swirling
back to the beginning
--- joining and re-joining
in a never-ending cycle.

Your soul now floats as if only a vapor
--- searching for reincarnation.

Only God, The Father selects the one
our soul inhabits next.

MAY TO DECEMBER

May to December,
their calendar days are waning.
The winds of change whisper
of horizonal things.
Too short the time
they were together
in their season of delight.
Slowly the first frost slips in
as summer hearts grow cold.

During the deepest moments
of their intimacy they were consumed
in the fire of passion
--- but will they survived the flame ?

SEPTEMBER

September.
A fragile time as life moves more slowly
and autumn branches
are ablaze with colour.
September.
Time now to take stock
of the spell cast by summer love
--- to see if it will survive the winter.

Cold, chilling winds will blow,
but warm hearts will keep love aglow
as the unadorned trees
take on a ghostly silhouette
and snow begins to fall.

Summer love --- September --- survival ?

RETURNING TO THE GARDEN

When mankind walks once more
*   to pleasure God's eye*
*   --- peace will resound throughout*
*   the world,*
*   and the garden will bloom again*
*   where Eve was once tempted.*
The serpent has slivered away
*   into its dark domain*
*   never to return.*
The trees will bear sweet fruit
*   for the taking*
*   and all will be well.*

HOPE'S GARDEN

Stop, listen,
hear her cries of desperation.
Her garden, once in full bloom,
now only weeds cover the ground
--- overgrown
with anguish and despair
from the lack of nourishment.
Still she holds on
to that little patch of lilies in the corner
where they will strew her ashes.

She needs to return to her garden
--- till the soil, replenish the seeds
to be pampered and cared for
so they will grow
--- beautifully blooming.

Those days of sorrow
and desolate nights --- will turn to joy
when she finds God's gentle hands
will help her turn her dreary garden
into her promised land.

*

GARDEN OF SORROW

Some of us dwell in a garden
so steeped in sorrow
that only dark flowers grow.

GHOSTLY VOYAGERS

A bronz'd sunset dims
along celestial shores
--- eventide unveiled.
Mist and shadows creep
across the dunes.
Ghostly voyagers plow the night
through the wilderness of dark
--- searching to find tomorrow:
moon and stars their only guiding light
across the cosmic sea.

JOURNEY LOST

In my boat a-rowing,
don't know where I'm going
--- following the river flowing,
as the birds to the south,
                    are soaring.

Caught up in the winds of change,
like tumbleweed on the open plain.
I lost all directions
--- going in all directions.
Lost all my connection
--- trying to find perfection.

I found myself
out standing in the rain
--- thought I had gone insane.
Still, I'm trying to find my way back,
back to life again
--- and this time
I don't want to miss the train.

A LUSTFUL LIFE

A lustful life: the intensity of its desire
will lead you to that burning fire.

Satan will use his snares
and lure you into an endless night
--- full of shadows and mist.
He will drag you down until you reach
the bottom pit of hell.

May the Lord forgive you your trespasses,
put out the fire of desire
--- your heavy heart to heal
and bring you into His eternal light
--- consume you in His loving flame.

LOST IN THE CITY 1929

She was a lonely bitch
--- discarded, a "child" of the city,
walking the streets
wet and shivering,
trying to survive the night.
Without food or shelter,
sleeping in back alleys
--- a reflection of the times.

I picked her up in my arms
and she licked my face,
wagging her tail with joy,
for she knew at last
she had found a friend.

QUIETUDE

1.
Nowhere to see you
--- nowhere can I hear your voice.
My life, running deep
in the memories of you and I
--- and those memories
calm my hectic days.

2.
There is a stillness
that befalls me
during my most trying times
--- when my heart is open
to reflect on the memories of you,
and that comforts me
during these solitary nights.

WHIRLING DERVISH

Whirling like a dervish,
spinning drunk with a love
that allows my heart to dance.

From the beginning,
when I took her in my arms to dance
--- we flew through love's cosmic night
to our joining among the planets.

Now in love, two "dervishes"
dancing far beyond the earth and moon
--- ever whirling, ever swirling
in the cosmic night.

WHEN

When you looked for beauty in the world,
    you found her.
When you searched for peace,
    she came into your life.
When you was alone,
    she brought you comfort.
When you sought refuge,
    she offered you shelter.
When she is near,
    love surrounds you.
When you are together,
    it brings you great joy.
When you dance,
    she is your energy.
When you are awake,
    she is your life.
When you sleep,
    she is in your dreams.
When you concentrate,
    your thoughts are all of her.
When you write poetry,
    she is your inspiration.
When you love,
    you only have devotion to her.
When you hurt,
    it is her pain you feel.
When you cry,
    the tears you shed are for her.
When you are sick,
    she is the strength that makes you well.

When you need her,
    she is always there for you.
When you talk to God,
    she is in your prayers.
When God answers you,
    she is your hope and love
        --- God is your salvation.
When you are apart,
    your longings start again.
While you live,
    she will always be in your heart.
When you die,
    this undying love
        will carry you through eternity.

WINGS OF 'MORROW

My heart still beats in placid tones
with all the love that it imparts.
No one but I will ever know
the pain that is keeping us apart.

Bitter-sweet of heart --- soul in sorrow.
What will life bring
            on the wings of 'morrow ?

*

LONELY

The forest dark,
the desert dry
--- the ocean deep in tears.
The nights
have lost their luster.
The days
---no one here to share.

UN-FILLING

He is just a nothing,
*   left with an empty heart.*
Yet, it was true love
*   right from the start.*

She still has
*   her wandering ways,*
leaving him with nothing
*   to fill his wanting nights*
*   --- fill his lonely days.*

Nothing !

*

CHASING SMOKE

Their love flame extinguished
--- his discontent smolders,
curls and rises
leaving his vulnerable heart
chasing smoke.

TERAGRAM *

*You are one of God's
wondrous creatures .... STOP.
All he wished for and longed for
he found in you .... STOP.
Nothing has more power over him
than the love he has for you;
one touch and he is yours .... STOP.
Fulfill his wish, to his heart's delight .... STOP.
Do not repel his affections
--- touch him
and never look away .... STOP.*

* MARGARET spelt backwards

ALONE AND FREE

She was a daughter
who could not leave home
and he was a rover
who had to roam.

Out on the prairie
--- that is his home.
The freedom that prevails
--- luxury relinquished.
He lives in the saddle, his horse
is the freedom he rides.

He'd love to settle down
and make her his bride
--- but she is a daughter
who could not leave home.

On a mountain among the pines,
--- from spring 'til first snow
a little log cabin was built
with a warming fireplace glow.
She came that winter
--- was a heaven to him.

Now spring again,
and she has gone home
to meet her maker.
She took his heart with her,
leaving him once more alone
--- but not free.

SONGS OR NO SONGS

It is hard to write
what is in his heart
when all the great love songs
have been written.
Songs or no songs
--- every time he looks at her
his loving heart
writes new music.

*

SWEET VOICE

When the birds
heard your sweet song
they suddenly became silent.

Burt Quote:
"Music extrudes love
*   and love extrudes music*
*   --- what a beautiful pair."*

TEAR STAIN

The stain from the tears that fell
were imbrued in his heart.

Time has elapsed.

The stain, now faded
--- yet still there to remind.

Burt Quote:
"The mirror holds the truth
 we dare not reveal to ourselves."

HELEN

A tribute to Helen Keller. 1880-1968

From a tiny spot on earth*
  a bright light began to shine:
Helen, even her name means light.
Darkness darkens
  her sun-drenched world
  --- the silence, a roar
  in her young head.

At "Ivy Green" the sights
  and sounds were turned off
  --- before she could even walk
  or understand her mission in life.
Never to see or enjoy
  the shadowy oaks
  of her graceful birthplace
  --- only enjoy the fragrant flowers,
  the kiss of a gentle breeze,
  the warmth of a touching hand.

Imbrued with learning
  from "The Miracle Worker"**
  --- opened her inner-eyes
  and she escaped that silent,
  cold-dark prison to leave her mark
  on an apathetic world.

God chose her to live this way
* so she could see through life's veil*
* and enlighten our own existence*
* with her poetic voice*
* and incredible insight.*

* * Tuscumbia, Alabama*
**Annie Sullivan

WORDS

I use the word love to describe her,
because she is love.

I use the word hope, because
she has become my hope.

I use the word joy, because
this is what she brings to me.

Precious are the words
that describe her.

SMAILHOLM TOWER

On a rocky crag in Roxburghshire
a lone and majestic tower stands
piercing through the early morning fog
rolling under her feet --- blanketing
the cold and empty moor.
Stone and mortar reaching
for the warmth of the early sunrise
as it slips into view
and the changing shadows fade.

A 16th century sentinel[3] surviving time,
where once atop, watchful eyes peered
through the night, their sight
toward the border, searching for
English marauders and revelers
--- ready to set ablaze the warning torch.
Now, only the haunting sound of the wind
churns inside her hollow core, echoing
ancient times and the names
of those who dwelled there.
The tower still dominates "The Borders"
verdant landscape of woods and fields
and grassy paths that lead up to
Eildon Hill's triple-peaks
--- where timid sheep peacefully roam.
Her memory scrib'd by Scott's [1]
immortal hand in "Marmion"
and sets the battle scene
for his epic poem "Eve of St. John."
Turner[2] too, drew an artist's view
of her magnificence.

1.Sir Walter Scott 2. Joseph M. W. Turner
3. Built by Robert Hoppringill C.1400

TORWOODLEE

Through the wrought iron gates
and up the gray gravel road toward
the manor house I suddenly stopped
and climbed the cobblestone path
through the stately trees to a lofty knoll.
The stillness was broken by the fluttering
of doves as I approached the old castle
--- and there she stood,
almost lost and forgotten
with her medieval presence
--- her majestic tower still standing,
silhouetted in the early morning light.
The once-jewel of the quaint village
of Galashiels, her roots firmly planted
in the rich Scottish soil,
destroyed over time
by weather and decay.
Her facade, now crumbled,
where nobility was once greeted
at her door by the Lord of the manor
and his lady--- now lies in ruin
--- stone upon stone in a mass
of indistinguishable debris.
I walked along her vine-encrusted walls
and through a formal garden
that once flourished with an abundance
of flora and fauna --- now overgrown,
and where peacocks still freely roam.

As if walls could talk, I listened
and imagined her hollow halls still echoing
the gala evenings and festivities of the past.
Looking out the bare openings that once were
magnificent windows with sweeping vistas
of the lush Scottish countryside
and the ancient Roman encampment
on the hills nearby.
Nostalgia took me by the throat
as I journeyed back in time with fleeting
glimpses of yesterday.

Torwoodlee built by
George Pringle c.1600

LOVING WORDS

The poems come
  with such a rush,
    they set my head to spin.
It is with all
  these loving words
    I try your heart to win.
I start with a phrase
  and it goes to rhyme,
    paragraph
        after paragraph,
as if guided
  by God divine.
To say what is in my heart,
  and on my mind.

Now, I lay my pen
  down to rest,
    knowing I have done
    my very best.
So, when you finally know
  my love is true,
    I'll be here
    and loving you.

LAST LOVE

She was the dream
of a most precious love.
Now my heart resigned
--- lost for all time,
knowing her name
will never be joining mine.

My heart no more to cry
--- no more tears entreat.
My heart, ground up like bone dust
and scattered on the wind.

Long after my swan song is over
let her take my loving words to breast
and read them --- hoping
they will warm her heart
through nights of cold.

A NOTE TO MANKIND
Burt E. Pringle

There are superficial differences
in all of us here on earth
--- we have many and various religious beliefs,
languages and colours, but we are brothers
together on this planet --- the only one known
to retain life.
Our basic sameness should unite us
in a single purpose to perpetuate humanity.
We should relinquish the quarreling we have
manifested in the past and bring enlightenment
closer than man has ever experienced before
in order to avoid strife and suffering, and
receive the vast reserves of knowledge we can
obtain from our individual beliefs.
Savor the immense values we can learn from
each of our different cultures for the common
good of all of us.

We must still the mind and always look
for the positive in life so that humanity
can continue to exist --- making our tenure
here in life as meaningful as possible without
wars or conflicts.
Find the inspiration to dissolve our differences
and bring universal peace
--- obtain an ultimate love for all living things
and leave this world a better place
for those who will follow.

Also by the Author

POETRY My Never Ending
Dance With Words
ISBN No. 1-4120-0031-4

LOVE and SUMMER DAYS
FADE AWAY
ISBN No. 1-4120-1146-4

Share A Tender Moment
Includes
"We Walked The Heathered Meadows"
A poetic journey through Scotland.
ISBN No. 1-4120-6586-0

OF ROSES And Spilt WINE
ISBN No. 1-4120-6587-9

RED PENNED DIARY
ISBN No. 1-1420-6588-7

REMEMBERING YESTERDAYS.
IMAGINING TOMORROWS
ISBN No. 978-1-4269-3047-8

Order books online at www.trafford.com
or email orders@trafford.com

ABOUT THE AUTHOR

Mr. Pringle is a native of Savannah, Georgia who resides in Jacksonville, Florida. He is an artist, architectural designer and watercolorist.

His artwork is included in many private and corporate collections and the official Florida Bicentennial book "Born of the Sun" contains two of his paintings.

He has published many volumes of poetry and his work is included in several anthologies and on spoken word CD's.

His biography is included in Who's Who in American Art, Marquis Who's Who in the South, The Cambridge (England) Dictionary of International Biography and is also included in International Men of Achievement.

He has designed several United States postage stamps and has received 21 Honorariums from the United Nations for his graphic postal designs. PBS/WJXT produced a half hour segment about his graphic designing.

Burt is also an accomplished ballroom dancer.

N.N. Wood